In the Beginning God
Created the Heavens...

The Moon

The Bible Tells Me So Press

In the Beginning God Created the Heavens...
The Moon

A children's book produced by
The Bible Tells Me So Press

PUBLISHED BY
THE BIBLE TELLS ME SO CORPORATION
2111 W. CRESCENT AVE, SUITE C, ANAHEIM, CA 92801
WWW.THEBIBLETELLSMESO.COM

First Printing March, 2018

Ever wonder what that big, bright ball
    way up there in the night sky is?

It's the
moon.

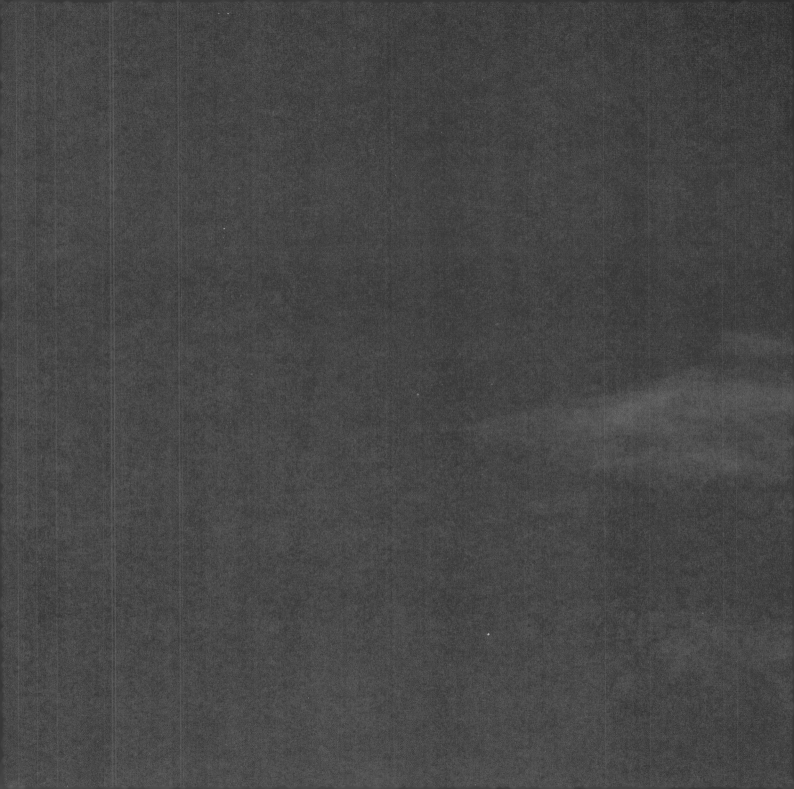

The moon is not up there by accident.

God created it
and placed it in the right spot
just for us.

This is what the moon looks like from space.

And this is what the moon looks like on its surface.

The large holes on the moon are called craters.

Craters are formed when meteors like this one hit the moon's surface.

up in space,

It actually does not make any light of its own.

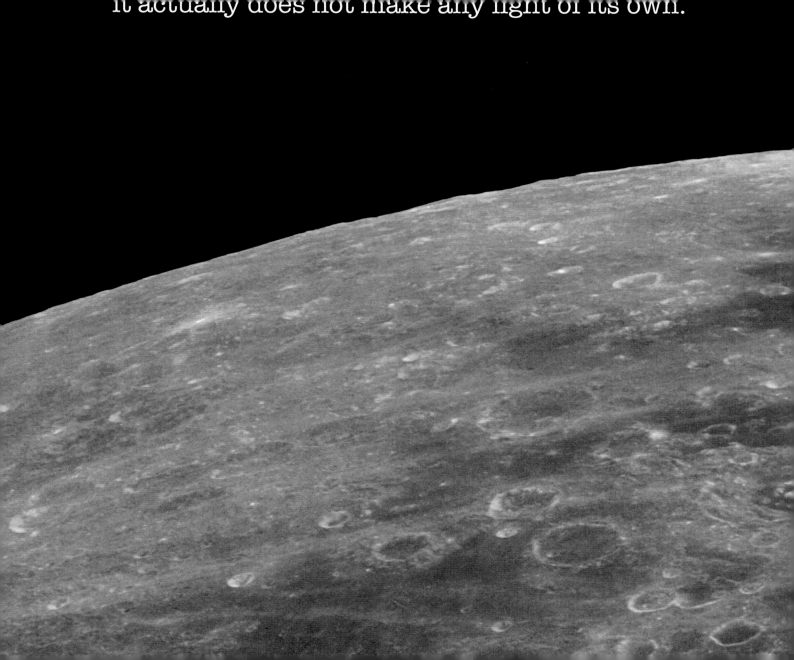

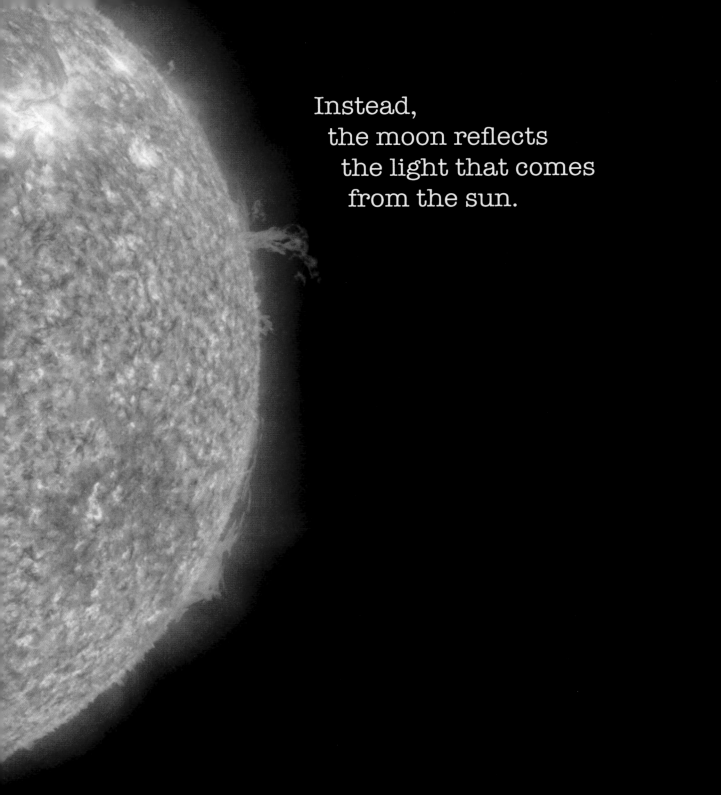

Instead,
the moon reflects
the light that comes
from the sun.

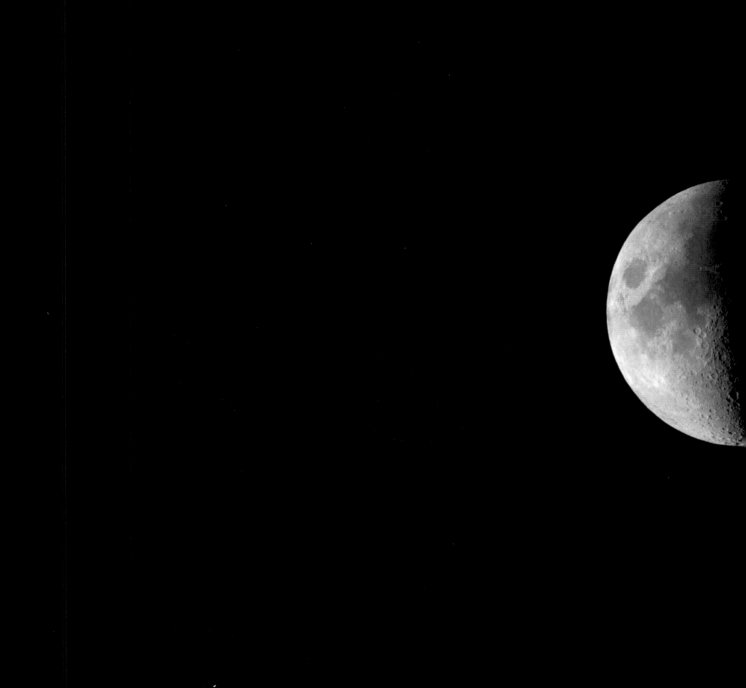

This makes the moon
the brightest object we can see
in the night sky.

Often a part of the moon looks
as if it's missing.

That part
of the moon is still there.
We just can't see it
because the light of the
sun is not shining
on that part.

The part
of the moon that
faces the sun is bright,
while the part of the moon
that is hidden from the sun is dark.
We can only see the part that the sun shines on.

Just like the earth,
the moon is always moving.

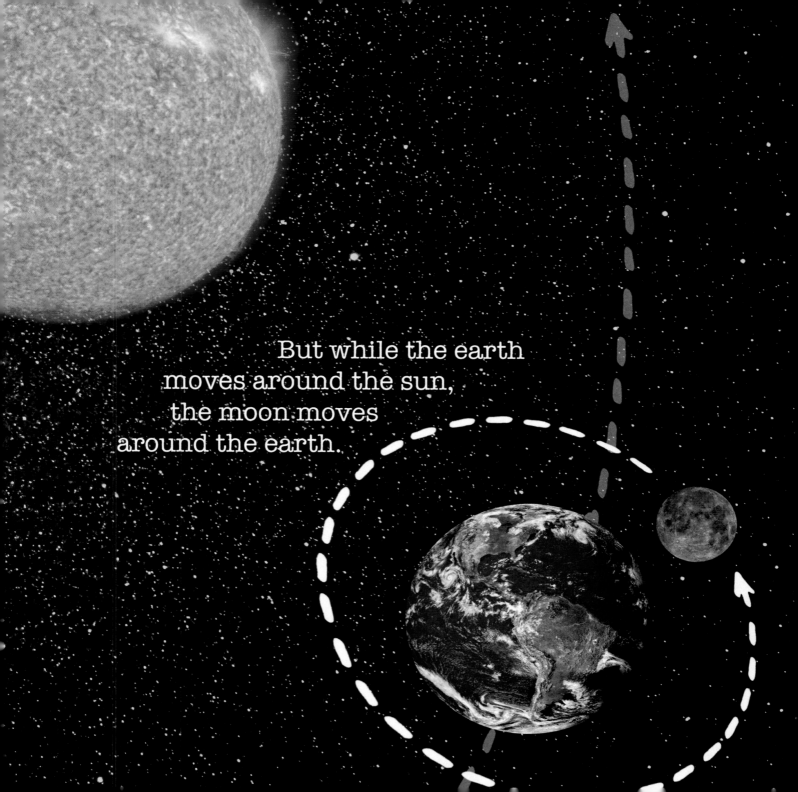

But while the earth
moves around the sun,
the moon moves
around the earth.

God made the moon in a special and beautiful way.

That's why we love
to look up at that
big, bright, and beautiful
ball in the sky—

the moon,

which God made for us.

Thank You, Lord!

The day is Yours;
the night also is Yours;
You prepared the moon
and the sun.

Psalm 74:16

For more
books, videos, songs, and crafts
visit us online at
TheBibleTellsMeSo.com

Standing on the Bible and growing!